THE
LOVE
BETWEEN

THE LOVE BETWEEN

Bridging the Gap Between
God and His Love for You

TIFFANY HAYES

COOKE HOUSE PUBLISHING
WINSTON SALEM

THE LOVE BETWEEN
Copyright © 2016 – Tiffany Hayes

All rights reserved. This book is protected by the copyright laws of the United States of America. This book may not be copied or reprinted for commercial gain or profit. The use of quotations or occasional page copying for personal or group study is permitted and encouraged. Permission will be granted upon request.

Unless otherwise identified, Scripture quotations are from the King James Version. Copyright © 1982 by Thomas Nelson, Inc. Used by permission. All rights reserved.

Soft cover ISBN: 978-0-9979923-4-2
eBook ISBN: 978-0-9979923-5-9

Library of Congress Cataloging-in-Publication Data
Names: Hayes, Tiffany
Title: The love between/Tiffany Hayes;
LCCN: 2016954008
LC record available at https://lccn.loc.gov/2016954008

Cooke House Publishing
(a division of Cooke Consulting & Creations, LLC)
Winston-Salem, NC
publishing@cookecc.org

This book and all Cooke House Publishing books are available at Christian bookstores and distributors worldwide.

Printed in the United States of America.- First Edition

Dedication

First and foremost I will like to thank God for placing the desire in my heart to write The Love Between.

To my husband who is so caring and loving, thank you, honey, for encouraging me throughout this process. I love you more than words can describe.

To my little boy, mommy loves you.

Thank you to my pastors, Mr. and Mrs. Hammond, my Mom, Dad, and Step-Mother. Not everyone is blessed enough to have as many parents as I do, and I count it a privilege.

To my siblings, thank you all for your support. I love you all, and thank you for your support.

A Message from the Author

My prayer for this book is to encourage and inspire you. I pray that the words on the following pages will trigger something in your internal being to want better than the past so that you will strive for betterment in your future and share the love between Christ and you with others.

—Alabasters Box, T.H.

Contents

Introduction   9

Chapter 1   11
Where it All Began

Chapter 2   13
The Love Challenge

Chapter 3   17
Freedom in Expressing Weakness

Chapter 4   21
Letting Go of the Past

Chapter 5   25
The Transformation

Chapter 6   29
The Love Test

Chapter 7   33
Freely Share

Chapter 8   37
Positive Thinking vs Godly Thinking

Chapter 9   41
Am I Worthy of Forgiveness?

Chapter 10   45
The Core Alert

Chapter 11   51
Help is Near

Chapter 12   53
Getting to the Root of the Matter

Chapter 13   57
Where Does Your Belief Lie?

Chapter 14   61
I Want to be Free

Chapter 15   65
Breaking Bread with a Judas

Chapter 16   69
Prideful Distractions

Chapter 17   71
A Call for Repentance

Chapter 18   75
Consistent Growth

Chapter 19   77
The Love Quest

Foreword

Mankind was made for love. Many would agree with this assessment, however, the concept of love has eluded mankind for eons. Giving love is equally important as receiving love in human relationships. Too often, this love has suffered by way of poor or inadequate interpretation of its authentic meaning from individual to individual. The ever growing pursuit for real love has driven many to social dating sites, newspaper ads, and the like. Though some results have proven to be successful, many have led to deep torment of the heart, emotional distress, and paralysis of living.

The Love Between provides courageous insight by the author as she unravels the drapes of the inner sanctum of her heart to reveal the truth of her personal discovery of self and love. May you find personal revelation, understanding, forgiveness, and healing as you explore the contents of this book.

God bless.

Kevin L. Hammond
Founder & Senior Pastor
13th Disciple of Christ Church

Introduction

The Love Between, is a book filled with many stories from my personal journey with God while experiencing His love for me. We will discuss and decipher many feelings to find the continual truth of God and be emerged by God's love as we take this journey through this book. And if you are like me, you, too, have experienced moments of pain and feelings of loneliness along with moments of triumphs and victories. My hope is that by the end of this book, we will move in a consistent flow of God's love, that you surrender your whole being to God and love like you never have before.

1 Corinthians 13:4-8 (NIV)

4 Love is patient, love is kind. It does not envy, it does not boast, it is not proud.

5 It does not dishonor others, it is not self-seeking, it is not easily angered, it keeps no record of wrongs.

6 Love does not delight in evil but rejoices with the truth.

7 It always protects, always trusts, always hopes, always perseveres.

8 Love never fails. But where there are prophecies, they will cease; where there are tongues, they will be stilled; where there is knowledge, it will pass away.

Chapter One
Where it All Began

One morning stands out more than the others when I was a little child sitting in church with my grandmother. That particular morning tears rolled down my cheeks as I witnessed others going to the altar for prayer. I believe I was 8 years old at the time, although I may have been a little younger. But what I remember most were the tears that fell while witnessing God move in so many lives. I recall one of the church members turning around to ask my grandmother if I was okay, because of the sobbing. My grandmother responded saying, "Yes, she is okay." I believe my grandmother understood what the Lord was doing in my young, tender heart at that moment. I didn't understand then that I was experiencing the love of Christ for His people through my tears. Witnessing so many people go to the altar for prayer and deliverance spoke volumes, and is a reminder that God is always with us with open arms.

As a child I gleaned from older women of faith. I enjoyed sitting at the feet of elders while listening to their life stories, battle experiences, and accomplishments. Through every story shared, the constant theme that flowed throughout was the love between them and God. Just like my grandmother, these elder women sought after God with every fiber of their being and didn't mind sharing their testimony. Many of these women have now gone on to heaven, but much like them, I also hold God very close and seek after Him. As a woman today, I'm still overwhelmed by God's love for His people, the kindness that He extends to us, the continual forgiveness that He offers to us, and the lessons learned through each process in such a loving way. I've learned through life that there are some things that happen at no fault of our own and I've learned that there are things that are simply out of our control. But in every lesson, there awaits the perfect opportunity to become closer to Christ and to trust Him with our lives. From the child in church sobbing sitting next to her grandmother to listening to those who have journeyed before me, what was once heard as a fascinating story has now become a life staple for me today. When we experience God for ourselves and believe the true unaltered and unconditional love between Christ and His children, we can never be the same because the love between Christ and His church is unfathomable and has the power to truly transform us if we allow it to do so.

Chapter Two
The Love Challenge

I would like to say that I have mastered this love walk from my first encounter of God's love, but that wouldn't be truthful. Like many of you, I have had many downfalls and moments where the love of God did not shine through me like it should. Although I desired to imitate the same love that God showered on me, I found it challenging to receive His love in the same way He poured it on me. There have been times I doubted who I was in God. I started to ponder if I ever understood who I was in Christ. And where the doubt rested, the negative thoughts soon followed. Although I wanted to believe that God loved me unconditionally, my voice was louder than the truth. But I can remember leaning on the stories I had heard from other great women and attempting to apply what I was taught. The more I applied what I was taught, the more experiences of God's love I encountered of my own. However, I still had questions. How can someone give continual love without experiencing continual love? At that moment I realized why applying the stories I had heard didn't work. It was because I'd skipped many steps to get the desired result of this continual, ever-evolving love walk. Then I thought that I could still maintain control of my life, but call it trusting in God. What I understand now is during life's journey we will be presented with a lot of teachable moments, as my mother-in-law says. And although it is tempting to apply the same approach to what seemly is the same scenario based on what you heard or experienced before, sometimes you cannot. The experience of love is important in life and without it we are a resounding gong, and that was precisely who I was.

Intellectually, I knew that God's love is perfect, and because of that I attempted to present a perfect picture of God's love without a real change of heart. Although I was moved when others were delivered and could feel the presence of God, that wasn't enough. I was not engulfed in the Holy Spirit, but by what I thought the love of God should look like. Sadly, I know that I am not the only one. Regrettably, I have spent many years of this journey acting the part instead of actually being the love of Christ. During this journey, I had to face the absolute truth of who I became and not who I wanted to believe I was. Fortunately, my heart desire is to be like God and to love like He loves.

Although the revelation of my Pharisee-like behavior was frowned upon, my desire for God drove me into the refining state of perfection. I no longer wanted to live off of my yesterday experience, but I desired a deeper fellowship with God. I knew that I needed a change, and not another alteration to my behavior but a true heart change that will accurately reflect the love between God and me. With this change of heart every relationship would be changed for the better because love never fails.

However, after receiving the revelation that I needed a true heart change, I proceeded to love and share the love of Christ using my own interpretation of how God's love should feel. Because of that I encountered many bumps and bruises, a lot of emotional wounds, and heartbreak because what I thought should have been received was not and what I thought I should have felt I did not. I thought that every encounter to share God's love would be received with open hands, and that I would be thanked for sharing it, but that was not always the response. Over time my heart started to become hardened. I'd developed many internal walls and controlling mechanisms to keep me safe, so I though. I'd tried so hard to keep a smile on my face, remind myself of who I am in Christ and my desire to please Him, but the more the hurt grew the more callused my heart became. Before I knew it, I became the resounding gong again. Instead of me talking to God about how I felt, I decided to keep my feelings within while continually serving the people of God. I became easily angered, easily offended, and hatred set in my heart. I was hurting, smiling on the outside, and suffering within. But I ignored the problem and hoped for great outcomes instead.

My prayer became:

Father, love is not weak or passive. It's bold and active and transformational. Through love You changed the world. Through Your love please change me. I want to love others with this brand of love—patient, kind, humble, enduring and never ending. Help me to start with this: when my emotions flares and triggers are pushed, please help me to believe the best outcome and think on those things that are lovely, and praiseworthy. When I feel irritated, please help me to see the other person as who he or she is becoming by your grace. Because You first loved me, help me to love others. In the name of Jesus whose love never ends, amen.

Chapter Three
Freedom in Expressing Weakness

Time went on and I thought that holding on to the bitterness that I harbored would aid me in not allowing myself to get close to others. I constantly reminded myself of the pain that different situations caused and the feelings that accompanied them. I thought if I didn't generate some kind of coping mechanism I would soon feel the pain of a hurting heart again. My natural reaction is to retreat, like a puppy who's reprimanded by his owner, who goes away sorrowfully, whimpering and afraid to come out of hiding. There I was, afraid, trying to avoid the very thing that I needed which was the love shared between one another. I must share with you that the desire to love was still burning and burning with a vengeance. I knew that in an effort to love again, vulnerability had to be my middle name. Vulnerability causes one to be open where they have to let their guards down in spite of their feelings. Honestly I was not ready for that type of vulnerability, so I stayed internally tight, not allowing any airway for God to have free course within. I thought that taking this stance would not allow love to seep out, so that I could prevent pain. What I soon learned is that the pain was still within and controlling my body language and mental reactions. The pain lived within because I held on to it. In my control, I rested on the pain, turning my ear away from God's voice. I rested in the pain as He continued to prompt me to forgive and move on. My silent response was, "But didn't you see what they did?" I felt vindicated and justified by the anger I held on to. Because I rested in the pain, my desire to control my reactions was empowered by retreating from others and controlling each reaction, because I knew that the love of God within me will seep out and the possibility of being hurt could resurface because God's love outshines anything that I could ever dream.

Interestingly, when I heard sermons about bitterness and unforgiveness, I would have never thought that I would fall into that category then. I knew that some relationships in my life I needed to forgive. What I didn't realize was that the walls I'd built as a safe haven had caused so much damage in many relationships around me and that bitterness had taken root watching others grow and blossom in friendships. These things I sought after but didn't want to become vulnerable to obtain them. I stayed on the shallow end of many relationships while continually asking God why I didn't have deep-rooted friends. As time continued I realized that the answer to this question was found in my actions to moments of true vulnerability. To be honest with you, I actually frowned upon sharing moments of weakness with others. My belief was that those things should only be discussed with Jesus or your spouse only. I didn't see the real significance of having friends. All the while I longed for that closeness in another sister in the faith. Unfortunately my thought pattern was far from how God intended relationships in the faith, but because of the strongholds in my mind, it was tough for me to open up to others. I couldn't remain tight and be vulnerable at the same time. It was not until I released the need to control each move inwardly and outwardly, that God changed my life and heart, and continues to do so. I had to change my perception of weakness, and understand that in my weakness God's strength is made perfect.

Chapter Four
Letting Go of the Past

Let all bitterness and wrath and anger and clamor and slander be put away from you, along with all malice. Be kind to one another, tenderhearted, forgiving one another, as God in Christ forgave you.
Ephesians 4:31-32 **(ESV)**

I was taken advantage of as a child and experienced a lot of emotional turmoil. I struggled with the thought of being free to love like Christ loves but held onto the blanket of fear which prevented me from doing so. Even so, I desperately wanted to be emotionally stable. I wanted to be loved, share love, and give love. But I was reminded of my past so many times in my effort to step out and share the love of God. I then found myself at a crossroad. There I was with a desire to be mightily used by God, but wasn't open to be used by God in all His magnitude. I didn't believe that God could take my fear and turn it to joy. I didn't believe that He would protect me from past hurts, after all how could God use someone like me. I thought less of myself than anyone else, so any negative words spoken only served as a reminder to how I felt about myself. I couldn't see the forest from the trees, meaning I didn't see that there was more to me than the story of my past. Many times, I thought that the mental blocks that I had grown accustomed to would never go away, and I would never be healed.

During this time in my life I'd become overly stubborn, arrogant, and prideful. I studied the behavior of the people that I wanted to be like who had obtained the material things that I wanted, and believed that if I wanted what they had, I had to do what they did to obtain those possessions. Now I understand that this was another effort to change who I was because I felt like I didn't have what it took to be the person I desired to be. After all, I was overweight, I wasn't the smartest in my class, It didn't have the cutest clothes, and I was consistently joked in and out of the classroom. I felt as if there was so many others that were better than me and many talked and joked me behind my back. So I thought how I could be Tiffany and obtain all that I desired. All the while on the inside, I desperately wanted love and I wanted to be loved out of my mess, out of the thinking that I'd grown accustomed to but it was extremely hard for me.

This mental state from the past followed me to my adulthood; the only difference is that I was no longer in the classroom but in the workplace. The jokes were no longer jokes but instead represented truth, yet I still wanted to share the love of Christ even with all the baggage I was carrying. Unfortunately, because I attempted to move forward without working on the wounds of my past, those same old familiar feelings resurfaced with every offense. One would say that the love I gave was conditional, and I would have to agree. Because I didn't know I followed a rule book that was made up of religious do's and don'ts and full of carnal thinking. However, a change was on the horizon. I had to learn how to release the pain to be free and believe what it says in ***John***

8:36: *" So if the Son sets you free, you will be free indeed"* (NIV). Sometimes, we have to continue to remind ourselves of the freedom that we have in Christ, to truly accept the freedom. In any unpleasant experience, it has the tendency to make you feel as if you're not free, but the if we focus on the truth of God instead of our feelings, then we will know without any doubt that we are free, and walk in that freedom. But I must share with you, this is a continual process for me.

Galatians 5:13 says,

"For you were called to freedom, brothers. Only do not use your freedom as an opportunity for the flesh, but through love serve one another" (ESV).

Chapter Five
The Transformation

There I stood in my kitchen. I remember like it was yesterday as I cried out to the Lord. I was directed by the Holy Spirit to give my cares to Christ, but I hesitated. I believed that if I gave God my bad attitude and my hot temper, I would be taken advantage of. People would think that I was a push over. I found comfort in ungodly fruits such as pride, selfishness, haughtiness, and bitterness. But in an act of obedience that evening I released my cares to Christ. I realized that all of those things that I was carrying were all bags of unforgiveness, as I hadn't release past pain but simply covered the issue and continued on with life without skipping a beat, until it was called out that evening. I allowed myself to be weighted by fear topped with self-sabotage, self-control, and a limited religious self-righteous life. I realized that I feared the vulnerability for others to see me just as I was, fragile, afraid, and lonesome. I knew that what I needed was love—the love that will love in spite of anything that I do or even think—and that is the love of Christ. I realized that the many attempts before to be loved and receive love was not a God centered love, but a love that I sought to fill a void, when in fact what I was needed was a true heart change in order to love as Christ does. On that day, I believe I started my quest for true love, the love that only flows from Christ while understanding the love between Christ and his children. I began to ponder on the process of love, the revolving cycle of the pain that is offered for love, the sacrifices that love requires, the forgiveness that love needs to flourish, and the hurdles that are crossed to love. My mind goes back to Christ and His suffering on the Cross for us because of God's love. Questions began to flood my mind, such as why did He endure such punishment. Why did He give His freedom so that we may live? Why did he endure the mockery? As I thought on these questions the answer was simple but powerful: *LOVE*. I understood then that all I had endured, the pain, the healing, the stories that the women shared with me as a child, and the experience of pruning the ungodly fruits in my kitchen were all God attempts to remove the unfruitful things in my life so that what I truly desired would have the room to grow within, because love only flourishes when hatred, bitterness, unforgiveness, and other ungodly fruits are not present.

The word of God teaches us that God the Father, God the Son, and God the Holy Spirit is one. In the book of *1 John 5:7* it says, *"For there are three that bear record in heaven, the Father, the Word, and the Holy Ghost: and these three are one."* In *John 1:1* says *"In the beginning was the Word, and the Word was with God, and the Word was God."* My friend, I have realized that love is no emotion but an action, a determination, a nature, a lifestyle, and a decision. It takes guts to love as Christ loves. It takes sacrificing and crucifying the flesh to love like God loves. In *John 12:25* it states, *"Anyone who loves their life will lose it, while anyone who hates their life in this world will keep it for eternal life."* Proclamations have been made that the children of God want the life that God has intended for us to live, but we accept the process in parts, instead of embracing the lesson holistically. Now am I saying that we are not supposed to receive the lesson in parts? No. But what I am saying is that at times we decide for God instead of God deciding for us how much we can handle? What I have endured so far hasn't always felt good but it was and continues to be needed. When I allowed God to take me on this journey, it was a completed work instead of partial pieces.

Chapter Six
The Love Test

In today's time we often use the word love as if that word does not hold weight, and I must question if it really does in many cases. As we know that the origin of this word is used to communicate deep affection, however, we often use the word love to talk about shoes, our favorite outfit, cars, and things of like kind. But what is love? Many times we speak about the love of Christ within our Christian communities, or at least we should, but do we really know what this love is that we often talk about? Or is it just another descriptive word used to show how excited we've become over an object or feeling. You see when we share the love of Christ, experience the love of Christ and live in the continual state of love in Christ, what we once used the word love for no longer is used the same. I had to learn this lesson the hard way, as my love for a very close friend was put to the test one day as I was faced with the option to wallow in rather hurtful offense or to quickly forgive. While visiting a friend one day, I decided to share the hurtful story with her. I'm not sure if I just wanted to get another woman's perspective on this story as I had been telling the Lord and my husband this story and as always both God and my husband provided a solution, or rather I just wanted to talk and feel justified for what I was feeling. So in the middle of me sharing this painful story with her she said, "Do me a favor." I thought,

"What? Don't you want to hear the full story? I don't want to do you a favor. I want you to just listen to me, empathize with me, and tell me that I was right and she was wrong." She went on to say, "Turn to 1st Corinthians the 13th chapter." My immediate thought was, "Oh Lord, the love scripture." I was hesitant but in obedience I agreed. I opened the Bible, turned to the chapter, and started reading. As I was reading my friend closed her eyes and started reciting the scripture. After reading this scripture I didn't need a rocket scientist to tell me that I had accepted some major offense and that I truly had to put this love walk to the test.

I'd realized that instead of praying for this friend who caused me pain I complained to God about how it made me feel. I'd realized that I provided room for bitterness, resentment, judgement, and rebellion. I saw that I needed major repair on my love walk quickly. After reading that scripture I sat in conviction realizing that I'd fallen prey to the test that love brings at times. I had been cradled by my negative emotions and excuses. This lesson taught me that in order to love like Christ we must love unconditionally; we must relinquish the control to only love others when things are going well or when we are being flattered with sweet words. We must understand that we have the power to love when others are talking behind our backs, or when opposition is present. We don't have to justify our actions to carry a grudge. Many times our love will be tested, but the beauty of this is that if our eyes are on Christ then we would know that this is taking place because His love is perfect and when our eyes are fixed on Him, He is all that we see.

So when something arises that would have set us off before, it will no longer have the power to because we are renewed and refreshed.

I wish that I can say that once I read what is commonly known as the love chapter, I ran back to this friend and offered my apologies for becoming so angry with her and offered forgiveness quickly, but that would not be true. In fact it was the total opposite. But with time, God, and a determination to walk in total forgiveness in this area the sting caused by the pain has decreased. Yes today, I am not the same as I was before. However, even in this stance, there is a true decision that must be made every moment that feeling of offense attempts to arise: and that decision is to forgive, until it is fully forgiven. But in order to actually love, I could not say or act what was not in my heart but actually I have to have love within. This love can only be given by God, this love can only be shown by God and experience through God, nothing more or less.

Chapter Seven
Freely Share

Not many things are free in this world, but one thing for sure is the love of God. I wish that I would have remembered this fact when I became angry many times before. In my past I would hold back my love to others when I would become upset. Although this may sound very childish and very irrational especially for a Christian, it is how I lived my life and I share with you my experiences in hopes that it will help in some way. There have been times when I became so stubborn due to anger that I withheld the love within because I felt as if the other person did not deserve the love that I offered. But the deeper I grew in God, the more this question resurfaced: Will you take the gospel to the ends of the earth or will you stay in your four corners? Will you stay in your four walls, in your church buildings, in your civic league meetings – simply in your section of the world – or will you ring the alarm to be the voice of God, to be the arms of God, to be God's spokesperson. In *2 Corinthians 5:20* it states, *"We are therefore Christ's ambassadors, as though God were making his appeal through us. We implore you on Christ's behalf: Be reconciled to God"* (NIV). In order to freely share the love of Christ I could not hold on to this love that I am to share nor think that I am the person that decided who God's love will be given to through me. God reminded me of the importance of forgiving and this necessity is more for us than for the person needing forgiving. In order to share the love of Christ there must be a true and deep dependency on Christ. We must understand and always remember that God uses us, and expects us to share our concerns with Him so that he can handle them.

As ambassadors of Christ, God makes His appeal to win souls through us, but how can He freely move in our lives if we do not freely share the word of God and who He is, which is love. Throughout my life I have given into many ungodly emotions and behaviors so I know firsthand how emotional blockage can cause a delay in our mandate. For many years I shared the gospel and the love of God for what it says on paper, but that didn't allow my secret life to reflect the words that we are to follow, as I didn't freely share. Let me break it down this way: how can one share a living word as a dead vessel being used? I was that Christian that talked about the word of God and shared the word of God, but I didn't want to share my experiences as it relates to how the word of God moved in my life. My saying was "I don't want anyone in my business." Today, however, God is my business but if I were to stay in my old thinking I would not be able to freely share. I guess the best way to share my condition then is to say that my heart was sick. It was not until I chose to listen to God when He prompted me to share my experiences and not focus on how I would be perceived, but instead choosing to trust that God will protect me. Because of that I must stay in a continual state of openness and trust in God and not allow myself to become easily offended or angered from past emotional hurts.

I know some things that I share can sound shocking, but trust me if it's not you then someone in your circle may have experienced many experiences that I shared with you. The beauty of this is that we are never alone and someone else can attest to what we have been through, thought, and experienced, but how would we know that unless we share openly. I used to wish that I could understand life through the lens of another and share that gospel with others, but understanding the love of Christ for yourself is priceless. Yes ,truly understanding that God has forgiven you is priceless. Every single thing that I've done against His will has been forgiven! My God will forgive another as well, it makes your testimony all the more compelling, inspiring, and life changing. However if we decide not to share where we have been and others only see the after effect, one may feel as if they are the only person that has gone through that difficulty. However when we reach beyond our comfy circles, the word of the gospel will spill over to so many hurting and desperate people looking for a person with your sound, your experience, and your testimony. To be honest with you, this lesson took a while for me to grasp because I was concerned about how I would look to others if they really knew how I felt, thought, and knew all of my secrets. Because of this I didn't allow anyone into my inner space for a long time. But I came to a place where I didn't care what others said and that I was not going to be in bondage any longer. What we allow in our spirit will manifest outwardly. Thus we must be conscience of what we are building. We must work on self through continual prayer and seeking revelation from God while asking our Heavenly Father to assist us in becoming a better person.

Chapter Eight
Positive Thinking Versus Godly Thinking

There have been times when I wished for a great outcome instead of talking to the Lord about the best outcome, praying about it, and believing in faith that all will turn out well. I can remember as a child throwing pennies in the wishing well, asking for whatever was on my heart or whatever I desired at that time. Even as a teenager I believed that I did the same, but there comes a time when we stop throwing coins in the wishing well and take a stand and put the desire that's in our hearts in motion. When I was a child I use to play with a broken computer. I can remember thinking that one day I would be a successful business woman. I'd even generated a Yahoo e-mail account and dreamed I would have a big office. I didn't know how I was going to become the person I saw nor what line of work I would be in, but I knew that I would make a difference somehow. At the age of 18 the employer that I worked for closed the office locally and moved the service center to India. I can remember leaving that company with a smile on my face and anticipation in my heart. Some may have mistaken this jubilant attitude as positive thinking, but I know for a fact that it was not just merely positive thinking but the understanding that there was much more in store for me, so I stepped out into the world with a new hope and faith in God anticipating what was to come.

Now, I wish that I could tell you that I found another job the next day, but I didn't. In fact I was without a job for a couple of weeks which to some may seem short, but to me it seemed like months. There were times where I became so bored that my mind became idle and in return, I started feeling bad for myself, which is a place we never want to be in. But one day I picked up the newspaper, prayed, and asked God where I was supposed to go. After praying about where I was to go, instead of showing up where I would like to go, He answered my prayers. Soon after praying and receiving instructions, I got up, put on my clothes and went to the place He instructed me to go. I can remember sitting down at the interview table and being asked the famous interview question, "What made you apply for this position." I sat there and tried to think of a political way of sharing that I was sent there by God but nothing was coming to mind, so I responded, "Ma'am I believe God told me to come here." She said, "Oh He did." I replied, "Yes ma'am," and not five minutes had passed and I was hired on the spot.

That day started me in the career field that I am in now and enjoying because I knew that God sent me. This career has taught me a lot and because I know that God has guided me through each step I have the confidence that is needed to do my best. I no longer have to pretend, but the office I sought when I was a child is now the office in my home. I no longer have to play on a broken computer because God has blessed us with working computers. Please do not think that this is a moment of bragging as it is truly relishing in the glory and faithfulness of God. Many of us have dreams in our heart. We grow up and some go on to walk in the direction of their dreams while others do not. Some depend on God to accomplish what they see while others believe that thinking positive will aid them the opportunity to accomplish the dream they see. While both are essential, as you do not want to have a negative attitude while you are going into the direction or living your dream, thinking positive is not the only measure used to accomplish the dream that you seek, but a true dependency on God is.

Many times we are taught to "just" think positive, but our thoughts will only take us as high as we know. Godly thinking will take us beyond what we know. Positive thinking says this is what I can do, and I am going to maintain a great attitude until the goal is accomplished, but godly thinking is an ongoing elevated thinking that will produce great results as it not only changes your mind but your heart and soul as well. As we allow God to enter into our thinking, we will be engulfed by His thinking, transforming our mind to His mind, and in that love as He has loved us. Once our minds are renewed, we will be able to see clearly and live life to our fullest potential, leaving no stone unturned when we rest our eyes to go into eternity. As a babe in Christ— as some of the church community would refer to someone who has recently given their life to God—I sought to learn good thought patterns from those I saw on TV, people that I saw in passing, and people that I knew. My motto was if someone had more than I then they must be doing something that I am not. Because I judged from the outer appearance at that time,

I was susceptible to grabbing onto anything that appeared as if I needed it.

This action created wishful thinking, and I thought that if I just read the Bible I would just become the person I needed and wanted to be without renewing my mind. I surmised that I could just follow the rules. It was not until the Holy Spirit revealed to me that I was attempting to gain pure transformation through merely changing my thoughts and wishing for a positive outcome instead of surrendering and allowing God to build His way of thinking, as He desires that for all of our lives because He loves us so. He desires that our whole being is given back to Him. It is imperative that we don't read something once or twice and wish that the change will take effect, but it's a continual investment in our thinking that makes the difference. It's the belief that if we keep our minds on Christ Jesus then He will keep our minds in perfect peace. My stance isn't that we must think positive, but to think on God and His promises for our lives. Positive thinking and godly thinking are not one in the same, even though they are sometimes stated as such. Investing in them both, however, will harvest great things as a result.

Chapter Nine
Am I Worthy of Forgiveness?

While attending a women's conference one afternoon, the speaker instructed us to ask God for the very thing that was on our hearts. I started in a seated positon, but felt the need to kneel. I knelt down with my head in the seat of the chair. As I opened my mouth, what was released were the words "I am worthy." As I continued to speak what was on my heart, tears rolled down my face as I laid in the presence of God, as he ministered over me I felt the weight of condemnation, fear, and unworthiness lift off of me. Like many of us I know the scripture ***"Therefore, there is now no condemnation for those who are in Christ Jesus*** (Romans 8:1 NIV). Oh, how I recited this scripture many times while feeling down about a wrong action or thought. And although I wanted to believe that I was not condemned, I must share that I didn't believe it. I questioned how God could forgive me for what I had done, said, or thought. So instead of accepting God's forgiveness, I bought into the lie of the enemy of condemnation. This caused me to encounter countless ups and downs, peaks and valleys, and stagnation of growth in my Christian walk. It was not until I learned that accepting God's promise is accomplished through faith and discipline. His word does not indicate that we will not feel underserving and compelled to condemn ourselves, but that the truth is there is simply no condemnation and that it's okay to release ourselves from captivity and forgive ourselves because God has already done so. His love is what allows us to be the free agents we are today. However, although some things can be great intellectual facts of truth, at times it is hard to accept the truth. In this case, it was hard for me to do so. Interestingly enough, I have asked God to remove my free will so that I would not sin against Him. I knew then that it was a foolish prayer because that was asking God to remove what He has given us. But I so wanted to be free from the shame and heaviness that I felt and thought that asking for this would provide the peace that I sought.

While watching a ministry broadcast one evening, the question was posed to the audience, "How many people suffer from unforgiveness?" As hundreds of hands popped into the air, I, too, should have raised mine. I suffered from feelings of unworthiness because I didn't forgive myself for things that I have done. I felt guilty for the things that I'd said behind another's back, for displaying a bad attitude instead of sharing and showing love, I felt horrible for disrespecting my husband; I felt guilty for everything that I knew was contrary to what was right according to the word of God. I'd become weighed down so heavy because I carried the weight of my sins instead of casting them to the One who died for the very thing that I was carrying. As someone who has tussled with the thought of being forgiven by a Holy God, a righteous God and so many other names that we use to explain who God is, the very thought of Him forgiving me was unimaginable. I totally mistreated His people and I didn't even like myself so how could I believe a Holy God could love me. But this was the very thing that

The Love Between

God asked me for. He asked that I give Him the very thing that held me hostage and bound. You see, I tried to punish myself by rehearsing the wrongs that I'd done because I felt as if I deserved to feel the pain, but the truth is that I didn't because God didn't give the condemnation I felt. I realized that the unworthiness I felt was a direct reflection of the real issue of unbelief. I had a lack of trust in the Creator. It is in our faith that we will find total healing in this area, because without faith it is impossible to fully live a life free of guilt and approval without love.

I understand that situations happen in life that cause us to be vulnerable. However, we have to always be on watch because the enemy would love to use that vulnerability and have his way in our lives. But it is important that you understand that you are worthy—you are worthy to be loved, you are worthy of forgiveness, and you are worthy of the good life. You are worthy no matter what you have done. And even for those who have done something to you, you are worthy to be forgiven just as you were forgiven. There is absolutely no condemnation in Christ and is important to know that so you can live the life God has destined for you. You must understand the importance of worthiness so that you will not settle because you don't know the status that you hold as a child of God. This message is not about material possessions you can obtain but an internal awareness that you are more than what you feel, say, or do. And for those who have done things to you that caused you to question your existence, worth, and importance, release and forgive them as well. You don't need any of those bags on this journey of self-discovery and worthiness in Christ. ***Ephesians 4:32*** says, ***"Be kind and compassionate to one another, forgiving each other, just as in Christ God forgave you"*** (NIV). When we forgive quickly—forgiving ourselves and others—we release the many toxins that we've digested and live in the next level in Christ.

Chapter Ten
The Core Alert

How we feel and what we believe activates what we confess with our mouths. It is what we think and believe that dictates the path we take and the direction we will take to get to our destination. When we understand the core of the matter, we can properly feed the core what is needed so we will grow. As some physicians say, we are what we eat. What we digest will come out and this is especially important when it comes to our spiritual belief. If we feel off kilter then chances are we are off kilter. If we aren't aware of what is causing the uneasiness, it is important to seek God for answers, as our feelings are a direct reflection of what we are thinking. If we are thinking contrary to the word of God then we have digested something that our body system does not like. Our emotions are the vehicle that our thoughts steer. However, if our thoughts are not sound and firmly planted in God then what we stand on is sinking sand.

While visiting a colleague one Wednesday afternoon, she started to express to me that she felt as if she was going crazy. "Crazy?" I mused. As she started to explain, I realized that her feelings were familiar to those I had at one point in time. She continued to share that her relationship with God is going well, but she still feels disconnected. Earlier that morning, another sister in faith visited her and asked her was she investing time in destiny building. As she shared that with me I became so excited that I wanted to jump up and down in pure joy. She continued to say that she didn't know why the disconnection was there. She shared how she didn't want to do anything when she gets home other than sleep. She was even becoming disinterested in the goal that she was working very hard to complete. She has much potential but was seemingly in a pit and needed help getting out of that pit. A word from the Lord was what was needed. She needed to know that her destiny is much bigger than the pit and that even this moment could be used to aid someone else. It was clear to see that the revelation was powerful and inspired by God. Her problem wasn't lack of knowledge or revelation, or connectivity to God, but she allowed something to creep into her inner being that took away a great deal of energy, so much that she didn't want to move forward in investing in her work.

As I stood there in silence but with anticipation to share with her what I believe God laid on my heart, I positioned myself to receive as well. I knew that as God used me to minister to her, He would minister to me also. We all encounter moments of allowing the old ways to revisit our hearts and often act out in that manner as we attempt to make headway into our newness. I'm sure that we have found ourselves in a time where we are back to the old familiar ways, where we are in the sensitive state of wearing our feelings on our sleeves. But we have to assess what it was that got us back to this state—what did we allow in. We must deal with the core of the issue as that will alert you in the future when the old familiar attempts to revisit you. This is a visit that we can certainly do without, as we continue to walk in our newness. If not, our old ways will always hinder our continual newness. **Romans 6:4** says, *"were therefore buried with him through baptism into death in order that, just as Christ was raised from the dead through the glory of the Father, we too may live a new life"* (NIV).

You know there isn't a moment that goes by where we aren't in a teachable moment, because in every situation there is something we can learn. I found that in ministering to others, we are ministered to as well because God is imparting His words in us to be able to share. We find life in spreading the gospel. It is the pure unadulterated truth of and from God. **Matthew 4:4** says *"Jesus answered, "It is written: 'Man shall not live on bread alone, but on every word that comes from the mouth of God.'"* It is not natural food we digest that we find our spiritual energy and tenacity but by the word of God. Many times we seek natural ways to satisfy a spiritual matter. Spiritual matters will never be solved by our own knowledge and power but by God only. We must deal with the core issue first. It is the core issue that triggers the spiritual and natural responses. We deal with these matters by researching the scripture of the matter. I once heard a pastor say that he is not going to look up prosperity scriptures if he is having issues with anger. I chuckled when I heard that, but whatever the issue is you must find in the word of God what He has to say about it. Then it is important to seek God for revelation and understanding of His word. While you are doing these things, continue to meditate on the scripture for whatever the issue is until manifestation takes place. We must remember that we must remain open for God to guide us and move in our lives. Continue to trust in Him and release your faith to love and fall in love with God as He makes you over in whatever area of your life you seek His guidance.

Like my sister that I was talking about earlier in this chapter, in order to accomplish any goals or desire, we must change what we are digesting if it is contrary to the path we believe God has destined for us. This does include people, places, and things. It is important that we are mindful of what we listen to, what we watch, and what we invest in. I've heard before that your greatest value is what you invest your money into, but I believe the same is true with your time and even greater, your faith. Remember you are on earth for a greater purpose and whatever that purpose is, it should not come second but above all else.

I ask if you are dealing or have dealt with issues, what have or did you allow in? Whatever we digest is what will spew out in our words, demeanor, and in the manner in which we carry ourselves and treat others. It wasn't that my colleague didn't want to finish her goal, but it was because something entered within that didn't belong, and it took its toll on her. This affected her productivity by taking so much energy away from her. But even in the sleepiness the core problem still exists. Our core problems will not just simply go away, but we must do something about it. We must apply the word of God and continue to walk in His light, casting down every imagination, and press against the grain when the problem attempts to arise. Do not become bogged down by the cares of this world, but press and hold on to God, the author and the finisher of our faith.

Chapter Eleven
Help Is Near

While completing this project, I encountered many times that I thought that I didn't have what it took to accomplish what I knew I was to do. My husband, Solomon, who by the way is a rock and an awesome, strong and gentle man of God, pushed me to not procrastinate and continue to work. I found out the importance of having another in your corner during this time, as I have tried many times before to accomplish many things without the help of anyone else. It was during those times that I had unfinished projects. Now I am not saying that another is needed for any and everything that you do, but I am saying that God does use others to assist in accomplishing His goals. It is through connectivity that many things are done. It was hard for me to share with another that I needed someone. The last thing I want people to know is that I was in need. Thankfully I have learned that this was a form of pride. I have spent countless hours trying to hold my own burdens without releasing them to God or those whom He has placed in my life to help me because I saw needing help as weakness. Because of this, I found myself like the Israelites, taking much longer to a complete a task than it should have taken.

You see, my brothers and sisters, we were created to love on each other, speak a word of encouragement when it is needed, and to bear each other's burdens when needed. However, one cannot grow if they are staying still and one cannot walk soberly if they are drunk with pride. As mentioned earlier, my husband is a big part of this project because he held my hands and arms up during this time. He continued to encourage me and tended to our son while I stayed up to write. I understand that If I were my old self then I would have pushed him away and thought that I didn't need anyone else; I would have been blocked by pride and what I wanted instead of what was needed to be done. Sometimes we cannot see as clearly, but another can. I had accepted that I needed help on this walk, that I needed another to hold my hand and encourage me. I am convinced that we stumble and stagger at times because of the lack of those around us that can be our support when needed. This can only happen when we allow the Spirit of the Lord to rest upon us, as we cannot effectively help another if we are not freely open to be used. Any of us can succumb to pride and try tackle everything alone or we can choose to connect with others in love and help one another accomplish the goals that are in front of us. There is no question that we need each other in this Christian walk. We will need each other to love one another, as each person in the body of Christ make up one body, and in the body we have all that we need. I think that it is remarkable how the Lord has created a well-functioning body, one that is dependent on one another to move and have the fullness of life.

Chapter Twelve
Getting to the Root of the Matter

There have been many days I have spent in sadness and even loneliness although from the outside it appeared that I had a wonderful life. I used to live by my feelings and considered them truth because what I felt was real. I use to look down on myself and believed everyone around me had more than what I had. I used to think that I lacked knowledge of many things that I thought I should have known. I would exalt all others because I didn't feel worthy nor important enough. I used pride as a cover up to hide my true feelings of how I felt about myself. Don't get me wrong, I could see that this belief needed to change but I didn't know how to do that then, nor was I ready because from my perspective falsified confidence was better than showing my true colors of what I lacked. I use to dress up the outside appearance while suffering inside. I can remember my husband saying to me a few times, "I wish you could enjoy your life like I enjoy mine, I wish you could feel what I felt." I wanted so deeply to feel the freedom that he experienced, but I continued to sit in my feelings. Interestingly enough, I've learned that our feelings are merely a reaction of what is going on internally. It was not until I asked God to reveal to me what was happening within me that I could understand the bouts of sadness that I'd experienced. I questioned where did this sadness come from, why was I experiencing it, and how do I live without depending on my feelings to guide me. It was then that I realized that the root of many hurt feelings was due to unforgiveness. I experienced bouts of sadness when triggers of hurt feelings were pressed and I allowed myself to live in that time of pain longer than what was needed.

Instead of accepting the healing of God to heal what was hurt, I wallowed in the excuse of being a victim. In return, harboring onto those offenses turned into bitterness and caused a subconscious memory of all past pain, which is the reason I continued to fall into sadness and loneliness. Although surprising to accept, I came to understand that I was a bitter person. I'd walked around with smiles on my face, prayers on the tip of my tongue, but little did I know that my internal fall outs, my stubbornness to forgive quickly, and sitting in the seat in unforgiveness fueled the desire of bitterness. The more I fed this desire the bigger it became and the sadder I became until one day I became fed up with this cycle. I opened myself up to God so that He could make the change in my life and in my mind. Since that time I have grown more in love with God and the love that He shares so bountifully. You see, it is not until we see and accept what the root issue is that we can live in the free gift we have in freedom. It is important to get to the root of the matter because it is then you can see the seeds that were planted, uproot them, and begin to sow good seeds while allowing God to water the seeds so they will flourish. However, we must understand that this is a process. Once you allow the

Lord to reveal the root cause of some of your behaviors and traits, they won't just vanish overnight. The process will certainly make you stronger and increase your trust in God even more as you know it is Him who is holding you while He is refining you.

Chapter Thirteen
Where Does Your Belief Lie?

Sitting in the car one evening while my husband drove, I asked him why he had been so snippy with me and quiet. I wondered had I done something to him. He responded that he just didn't have anything to say. Now my husband is most certainly a listener more than a talker but this was out of the norm. I knew something was wrong but I didn't want to probe too much and become like the dripping faucet that the Bible warns against in **Proverbs 24: 15**: *"A quarrelsome wife is like the dripping of a leaky roof in a rainstorm"* (NIV). So I sat there immersed in my thoughts worrying what I have done to cause this reaction from my husband. I feared that if we did not talk about what issue was apparently present then we would soon be headed to divorce court. As the stories ran rampant in my mind, I became even more worried that this would not end nicely.

As I continued to stare out of the window, watching the asphalt on the road, the trees blow in the wind, and the homes as we drove 45mph down the highway, I continued to worry strongly. At this time in my life, a few others sisters had complained about my attitude towards them, as being standoffish and antisocial. Now for someone that is a pretty bubbly, charismatic person, that's a major red flag to others and me. So to have my husband act this way towards me worried me to no end. I wanted to know what he was thinking every moment and I wanted to know what I've done to deserve the silent treatment. One morning he put an end to my wondering. He shared with me that I have been hot and cold for a while and that he found that it was better if he stayed quiet rather than talk, because he didn't know what would trigger an unwelcomed attitude.

When he shared that with me, I felt awful, confused, and saddened to know that my husband—the man that I have been with for years, the one that I would stand on the roof tops to profess my love for him—felt as if he couldn't share with me because he didn't know which side of Tiffany he would receive. We had a problem that I didn't know how to fix, but God did. As I started my quest to be levelheaded in my actions, I was quickly reminded that this transformation must first take place inwardly. One must be changed inwardly before the outward manifestation is seen. This was a big job and I knew that God was the only one that could get me out of this downward spiral of conflict and self-doubt. I asked God to reveal to me what I was doing to cause conflict with so many people, including my husband.

During the time of seeking God as it relates to the recent reactions I realized that I was in a new place in my life spiritually, an unfamiliar place and I was downright scared. Instead of directing my concern to God I continued to do life as normal while spreading the fear that I felt within by way of ungodly tones and attitudes to those I encountered. Because of the sensitivity and the confusion of the fear that I was experiencing, I allowed myself to become irritated and saddened quickly which in turn caused offense not only in me but from me as well. I didn't know what was going on within me. I tried to correct the issue myself by acting the way I was supposed to act, but the fear that I felt from the spiritual refining place caused areas of concern intellectually because I could not make sense of where I was spiritually. I just knew that it was unfamiliar to what I had experienced before. However, instead of casting my concerns on God, I chose to respond with the fear. I had to come to a place where I grew tired and didn't want the fear of the unknown to melt away relationships any longer.

    It was time for a change and time to take a stand. I had to fight against the feeling of giving up because of what I feared. And when I felt as if the fear attempted to overtake me, I continued to surrender to God even the more. I became very specific in my prayers against fear and prayed for strength in that area. I knew after a while that what I once feared would no longer haunt me nor would it alter my attitude and behavior. But I had to truly trust in the Lord from the depths of my soul. I had to decide not to trust in the fear but rather trust that God has all things under control knowing that He gave me the power to speak to anything that is contrary to His word. So I decided to release my faith in the name of Jesus and speak to anything that didn't line up with the Bible. The relationships that were challenged during that time were mended, but although the relationships were mended they are not like how they were beforehand. That is okay because I trust that I and they are better people now than we were then.

What I once feared as the unknown is now embraced as the evolution of my life in Christ. I've learned that in every season of life, a true dependency on Christ is needed because each chapter of your life will have new features and any of them can be scary if you are not fully trusting in God. We must know with our whole heart where our belief lies. We must know if we are truly believing in what we see and feel or the truth of God. Many of us seek to be consistent in our emotions and in our thoughts, but find ourselves being inconsistent in those areas. I must share that in order to obtain godly consistency in these areas, we have to believe only in God and what He says and speaks over our lives. Because it is what we believe that will determine who we will become. I didn't believe that God was doing a good work in me when this newness within started and because of that I thought, believed, and acted out of fear. But when perfect love comes in, it will cast out all fear. In order to journey through this love walk, we must allow the lover of our souls to take residency in our temple here, now, and forever. When this happens we will no longer be joined to God in prayer and separate in actions, rather joined in prayer, actions, motives, and our whole being.

Chapter Fourteen
I Want to be Free

One day the Lord revealed to me different traits that I would display when I felt afraid, abandoned, or hurt. He shared with me that although my desire is to love and embrace others, when I become uncomfortable I distinctly revert into a prideful state. This revelation was given to me a little after I called my husband on the way to the gym one afternoon. As I waited for my husband to answer the phone I increasingly became more excited from the revelation that was given. When my husband answered the phone I shared with him that I realized that my sweetness was surrounded by thorns whenever I felt scared, abandoned, or hurt. The thorns were used to keep people away from the beauty they possessed because I no longer felt comfortable to share with others who I was. As I was sharing with him, I received more revelation and the more revelation I received the more astonished I became. I felt alive and free knowing that God had shown me myself and would also provide instruction for how to change in that area.

Oh, this was a beautiful occasion and I was ready to tackle this, not knowing that I would be tested so soon. My husband, being the listener that he is didn't say too much as I spoke. He let me share all the wonderful revelation that God had shared with me. After my workout, we talked all the way home and all was going well. But then an argument developed seemingly out of nowhere. It was an argument that left me standing in my kitchen with tears flowing from my eyes, face red, eyes swollen from the many tears and hurt feelings. I wanted to scream at him, belittle him, and tell him a major piece of my mind. I felt like throwing my wedding ring at him out of rage, but as I stood there with my hands in the dishwater all I heard was a song that I'd heard long ago and these words rang out, "I show love." At that moment I pushed my pride aside. I was still perplexed as I couldn't understand my husband's reaction from what was a remarkable day of revelation for me. Furthermore, I didn't believe that this time I had done anything wrong. I realized that as we walk down this path of righteousness, at times we are going to have to hold our peace, stand when we are wrongly accused, and fight for the accuser.

After I dried my tears and made the decision to show love in spite of the actions of my husband, that is when I began my healing process. It was at that moment that God showered me with grace and His love. At that moment my mind was clearer, my behavior was different, my old ways were not on display, and I was actually living God's way and not my own. In the past I knew that if I cried hard enough, if I pouted long enough, if I stayed quiet long enough, or yelled loud enough then I would get his attention, but this time in my distress I caught the attention of God. ***Psalms 34:18*** says, ***"The LORD is close to the brokenhearted and saves those who are crushed in spirit."*** As I continued to complete my housework I was standing on my own two feet in God as

The Love Between

He directed me how to move, what to say, and when to say it. For the first time in my life, I was free from the spirit of manipulation where I would yell to get my way, and instead I laid it all at the altar. You see the many emotions experienced in that small timeframe were all the feelings that I felt, but at the core was God shining the light on the true response, and that was to love in spite of how I was are being treated, love in spite of any disagreement, love in spite of how I feel—just love because I welcomed God into my heart and the power to forgive is present. It is when we have God that we have everything and are truly free in Him. As I finished my housework, God started sharing with me words to share with my husband—words of encouragement and love. I was so blessed by this because what could have been handled in a fleshly manner was filtered by God and an atmosphere of worship and praise manifested instead of discord. I believe that this is the stance we all take when situations like this arise. God took this same stance as He sent Jesus to the earth in the flesh to die for our wrongs and downfalls. God loves us no matter what we have done, He forgives us, and covers us in the love of Christ. Let's look to Him as the supreme example for our life.

Chapter Fifteen
Breaking Bread with a Judas

I don't know about you but I know when I think about Judas, I certainly do not wish to be associated with him in any way imaginable. Who does? Knowing that he betrayed Jesus was nothing that I wanted to be attached to. However, the more I thought about this story, the more I could relate to Judas I didn't accept the love that Christ died for us to have, experience, and share. I found myself betraying God by holding on to my selfish pride instead of helping another. I did not acknowledge Christ for all that He is. I didn't allow the word of God to penetrate the core essence of my being, and regrettably didn't expect consequences would be that bad. Just as *Matthew 27:1-4 says "Early in the morning, all the chief priests and the elders of the people made their plans how to have Jesus executed. So they bound him, led him away and handed him over to Pilate the governor. When Judas, who had betrayed him, saw that Jesus was condemned, he was seized with remorse and returned the thirty pieces of silver to the chief priests and the elders. "I have sinned," he said, "for I have betrayed innocent blood." "What is that to us?" they replied. "That's your responsibility."*

I am even saddened to think back to when I was in this state, as there were so many things I accepted instead of the love the Christ. I can remember being led so deeply by pride that I would reason like a mad woman to make sense of any decision I made that didn't line up to the word of God. After Judas betrayed Jesus, he realized he had made an unwise decision and attempted to return the money; however, it was too late. And like Judas what I thought was simple actually had a huge impact on my life. I found myself running to religion in an attempt to find peace. Struggling with the guilt of the sin of pride, I turned my nose up at others in an attempt to make me feel better about myself. I would minimize another's worth just to enlarge my own ego. I would speak that there was no condemnation in Christ and wanted to accept and receive the promises of God while mistreating His people. As time went on it was revealed to me that I covered my issues within with pride, ego building, and stepping on others. But I came to a point where I had to face my true self. I found myself in a pit of fear. I was full of religion but not relationship. Religion kept me bound, but it was a true relationship with God where I would find the abundant life that He wanted me to have. But it took a while for me to get to the point because I used God like an allergy medication—only taking His word and applying it to my life when the season called for Hm. There was a serious disconnect in my relationship with Him because I didn't accept the word of God in my heart.

One may ask how is it possible to spend so much time with Jesus and not believe in Jesus. It is similar to attending church five times a week but still not have a relationship with Him. We can pray to God and not have a relationship with Him; we can stand up and clap our

The Love Between

hands, do our church dance, turn around three times, sit back down and throw water over our left shoulder, but these things are simply religious antics that hold no power if a true relationship and belief in God is not developed. Just as Judas still questioned Christ even though he spent much time with Him, I found myself playing church. I said and did all the right things, but once met with a challenging matter, what I desired quickly faded by the cares of life. As quick as a snap of a finger, I found myself trading God in for a moment of worry, an hour of anxiety, followed by days of bad attitudes and hot tempered tones all because I lacked a true dependency on God.

    I wonder if Judas knew that he could experience freedom in God even after He betrayed Jesus. I wonder if he would have soon realized that he was not the only one that may question Christ at times, but to trust Him anyway. I wonder if he would have taken the time to think about Christ's teachings, would he had known that he too could have been forgiven. Did he know that Christ was going to die for him as well? At times our guilt can leave us captive, paralyzed by our faults, and when we think of the love of Christ, instead of allowing His love to free us, it makes us feel even worse. Like Judas we find ourselves reciting that we are not worthy, and in our minute thinking, we don't believe that He simply gives us the ability to live freely in His abundance. So before we judge Judas again, do an assessment of your life. If we're not honest and careful, there may be a Judas in us that only God can set free.

Chapter Sixteen
Prideful Distractions

From a young child I was challenged with the thought of believing that I didn't know as much as another, that I wasn't smart enough, pretty enough, thin enough, and the list goes on. While in middle school and the first couple of years of high school I was joked, talked about, and a lot of times I rode the school bus home in tears because of the treatment received in school and on the bus. Because of this treatment I grew up very insecure not feeling loved and not loving myself. Interestingly enough I didn't realize that the cruel treatment that I had experienced had dug its grip into the very core of my being until I was married with a child. It's interesting how God shields us until we are mature enough to deal with issues of the heart. As matters of my heart were revealed, I started to notice different coping mechanisms that I'd created to get through the day by day matters. I was hot tempered because I didn't know how to deal with the real issue. I became manipulative because I didn't know how to truly ask for what I wanted due to the possibility of rejection. I became prideful in an effort to build myself up and run away from all that I believed I was lacking. I found that I leaned on false comfort of coping mechanisms to avoid the real issue of my heart. You see I'd become comfortable in the state that I was in—prideful but believing that I was trusting in God until one day the wool was removed from my eyes. Truth be told, I was depending on my own strength, ability, and familiarity. However I did not have an experience with God for myself to know how to truly trust Him. This was something I yearned for because I saw the peace that others had that came from a relationship of trusting God. I wasn't there yet but I knew that God could and would help me. It was then that this love quest started and will continue until the day I die. I now understand that it is not a one-time revelation but a lifetime. My story may be different from yours, but we all must understand that no matter how our story began, it is important that we love one another as we all are members of the same Body of Christ, and that Body is made of love.

As I stated before, I would love to say that I was changed overnight but that just isn't true. There are times even today where I have to remind myself that my comfort is in the Lord. You see, when I allowed pride to be my comfort zone I was not open God's love. Today, I let nothing be a shield between me and God. As I grew and with the aid of the Holy Spirit, I came to the understanding that pride is used to distract us from the real issue. When we act in pride we believe that we know what is best for our lives and in return we then become distracted from our true purpose, our true identity, and the lesson we are to learn as we live on earth. My friend may I remind you that the enemy would love to distract you enough that you are not living the life that God has ordained for your life. He would like to blind your eyes from the truth of God's word. As I shared before, I found comfort in the prideful distractions, but when my eyes were open, I was able to see that what I found comfort in before was simply a mirage of lies. I admonish you to walk in the truth and be made whole.

Chapter Seventeen
A Call for Repentance

Repentance is defined as the action or process of repenting especially for misdeeds or moral shortcomings, whereas repent is defined as to feel or show that you are sorry for something bad or wrong that you did and that you want to do what is right. There is no shame in me sharing that I have learned some of my best lessons through the repenting process. I am also reminded of my son when he was 5 years old. My husband disciplined him and my son was professing that he will not do what he did wrong again. As his mom, I didn't want to see him crying, but I also knew that he needed that time to think about what he did wrong and reflect on the consequences for him to make a choice not to follow the wrong path again. It is the same with us, as **Hebrews 12:6** says **"Because the Lord disciplines the one he loves, and he chastens everyone he accepts as his son"** (NIV). The same way my husband disciplined our son is the same way that God disciplines us because He loves us. What a loving Father!

There have been many things that we all have done that we aren't proud of. Sadly in the Body of Christ, even after we repent and decide to follow the righteous path, what we did prior to asking for forgiveness still haunts us today. But how can one find true repentance without the fall, without the conviction of the wrong doing and without the love of God in our spirit? You see, some have learned that conviction is a powerful tool. Conviction occurs through the aid of the Holy Spirit whereby we recognize that there is a problem and we seek God to return to right standing with Him. There are also some that run away from the conviction process, knowing that something is off kilter but do not stop to acknowledge the magnitude of the problem. At times some can find themselves covering their sin by reasoning. Sometimes I marvel at the power of ownership. Accepting the wrong that we've done and accepting the forgiveness of a Holy God and moving forward is such an astronomical gift that not many people can fathom. Because of that some of us still hold on to the guilt and shame that separates us from the conscious connection with our heavenly Father.

As a young wife and dealing with the uncertainty of being a wife to my husband, I feared that we would not last until death do us part, as I had not seen many successful marriages early in our marriage. Although I wanted to be the best wife that my husband needs, I found myself hitting a brick wall when disagreements arose. I can remember one disagreement so vividly. During this disagreement I became so angry that I walked out of the house, stomped to my car, and sat there thinking that our marriage was over. During this time I was the more vocal one in our marriage and it did not take much to make me angry. All of the uproar that occurred was due to my behavior. After a while my husband came to check on me. By this time I was much calmer because I had time to process my thoughts, cry out to the Lord, and cry some more. When he came to check on me,

I was able to see the disruption I had caused and asked for his forgiveness for my behavior. I shared this story with you because sometimes we cannot see the flaws in ourselves in the midst of our wrong decision. Even if we can, we must remember that it is never too late to repent from our wrongs and turn from our ungodly behavior.

Understand that while we are on this love journey there will be times where you will have to repent from something that you may do, say or think, but understanding that it is never too late to turn from what you may do will aid you. Now of course we do not want to intentionally walk in sin, but if you stumble it is okay. Just keep moving in the right direction knowing that you have the saving grace of our Christ on your side. Repent from any and all wrongs you have done, choose to forgive yourself, and accept the forgiveness that God has already given you and walk on.

Chapter Eighteen
Consistent Growth

One day I opened my Bible without any particular scripture in mind and my Bible fell open to a familiar devotional that I read before titled "Perpetual Puberty." The devotional indicated how we are in perpetual puberty as we are steadily growing. As I read the devotional perhaps for the fourth time, I recalled thinking, "Lord why am I reading this devotional again. I get the point." But it dawned on me that my response to some situations were prideful. I apologized to God and attempted to keep the devotional at the forefront of my mind. However, I soon forgot the lesson because deep down I was insulted that I was still dealing with pride.

A year or so later, I was again reminded of that devotional. At that time in my life, I was fighting against the temptation to walk in pride. I was reminded that we are all in perpetual puberty because we are always growing and developing. So what was insulting to me at one point in my life became a source of strength and encouragement in another. I believe that if I had been walking in humility when that devotional was reintroduced the fourth time, I would have caught on then and not have to relive lesson. Nevertheless, I am grateful for the journey to learn daily because it is with the daily lessons that all of the scales of my sin nature are being purified.

So now with the knowledge that we all grow daily, it has made it easier to accept challenges to love. I know that even if I don't get it right the first time, that's okay because we are continually moving in the right direction. I realized that humility was the missing element in many of the challenges that I've encountered in life. I also allowed pride to rule in my life for many years and didn't notice. This lesson has been tested many times over and I'm sure it will arise again, but just as I am determined and devoted to God, I will not live in fear, pride, shame, or guilt but choose to live by faith, love, and humility. Yes, there are always times when I am tempted to give into the flesh and would be dishonest if I said I didn't fall anymore. But through the power of God, I know that I can get back up and continue on. I am reminded that each fall offers new opportunities to learn more about myself and Christ. We all must remember that this love walk between God and His people is not a sprint but a life full of twist and turns. Remain consistent in your faith knowing that all will be well. Stay humble and continue to love God and His people.

Chapter Nineteen
The Love Quest

Throughout each chapter of this book, I have shared lessons that I've learned from just living and my relationship between God and me. The beauty of the Love Between is that although these lessons were shared from my life, we all have lessons that we have learned and can share with others. Be open to receive from God and others. The truth is that we cannot journey through life alone, but there is power in our connectivity, our shared interests, and our love for God and each other that will keep us encouraged. Don't get me wrong, sometimes you may feel like giving up, but in times like that think of who Jesus died for and then think about the mandate on your life. You may not have to physically die to save another but we certainly have to die to self.

I've shared with you that I have been abused, I have come home with tears in my eyes, I hated myself, I lived in guilt and shame, I've had moments that I thought that my life didn't matter and that others would be better off without me. But like me, what God has called you to be cannot be stopped by your own faults or another's. We all have a purpose and it is through this purpose that others will draw closer to God. We must stay connected to God so that the love between God and His people will shine throughout the earth and all who are in it. However, when we hold on to hurt feelings, unforgiveness, shame, guilt, jealously, comparison, lack of confidence, a victim mentality, pride, selfishness along with so many other matters of the heart that we experience, we halt our abundance of purpose on earth. It can be hard. I have several reasons I could have turned away from this quest but the love I have for Christ is worth every trial and challenge. I decided to cast my net and pull others by the love of God. I choose to love others despite any abuse I've endure or will endure. I choose to love despite what is said or shared about me. I choose to forgive and live in peace with my Father—that is the love between God and his people. Love wins!

About the Author

Tiffany Hayes has been a motivational speaker since 2011, where she started walking in her calling as a radio co-host on The Voyce Radio (www.thevoyceradio.com). She then began writing and sharing morning devotionals to thousands of listeners on a local Hampton Roads, Virginia radio station, "The Word in Praise." Moving from behind the microphone, Tiffany has made appearances on the Trinity Broadcast Network (TBN) and other mediums where she has shared her own testimony. Tiffany also has her own online show called "Alabaster's Box with Tiffany Hayes," where great testimonies are shared with the world from both business and spiritual leaders, letting you know that if they made it, so can you!

She inspires and encourages others to transform and renew their thought patterns so they may live the life God intended for them. She is married to her "sunshine," Solomon Hayes, who she loves very dearly, and has one child, MeSiear," who she still calls her "baby" even though he is a growing 7 ½ year old boy. Tiffany lives a wonderful, fulfilling life and she accredits this victory to her faith in Jesus Christ and her persistency to never give up.

To contact the author for speaking engagements, conferences, book tours and signings, write

Visit www.thelovebetween.com
E-mail: alabastersbox@gmail.com

Other Authors by
COOKE PUBLISHING HOUSE

The Comeback chronicles the life of Pastor Darrin Williams, as told through snapshots of his life from boyhood to the present. It is a story of redemption and reformation as Darrin undergoes a complete 180 degree turn from the life of a gangbanger and drug dealer to one who fully established his belief and trust in God. He took the unlikeliest of life's circumstances and became a firm believer in God, showing that all things are possible to those who believe.
ISBN: 978-0-9979923-2-8

For more information, visit
www.fightwithmyfaith.com

Other Authors by
COOKE PUBLISHING HOUSE

I'm T.O.U.G.H is a 60 day devotional book intended to resolutely ground the reader in a strong spiritual foundation. The messages in this book thrust the reader to think and reflect on their own lives and situations and to dig deep in themselves and be contingent on the victor that is in each and every one of us. Through scriptures, stories, personal testimonies, and teachings, readers will grasp hold to the fact that they are built to last.

ISBN: 978-0-6922-0263-0

For more information, visit
www.imtoughdevotional.com

Other Authors by
COOKE PUBLISHING HOUSE

Devastated But Not Destroyed is a divine interruption for those who may be headed towards destruction. It will jolt your faith, sustain your strength, and change your perspective from one of pity and pain to that of power. Discover how to master the moments of your life, pack up the pity party for good, and embrace the challenge of change. Everyone at some point will experience devastation, and this book serves as the go-to guide to rediscover the tenacity and fortitude necessary to avoid the pitfalls of destruction.
ISBN: 978-0-692-34201-5

For more information, visit
www.devastatedbutnotdestroyed.com

Other Authors by
COOKE PUBLISHING HOUSE

We speak of spiritual warfare in the same mindset as physical warfare. We have approached it with thoughts of violent and vehement confrontations. In actuality, spiritual warfare is best fought using simple biblical principles. 100 out of 100 people are offended, the offender, or both. This book is intended to teach one of the most basic, yet most powerful principles - and that is the principle of forgiveness. As you begin to practice this principle, you will experience a freedom in your spirit that you have longed to have.

ISBN: 978-0-692-30523-2

For more information, e-mail
scvinson@gmail.com

www.ingramcontent.com/pod-product-compliance
Lightning Source LLC
Chambersburg PA
CBHW070549300426
44113CB00011B/1837